THE THREE KEYS TO TEACHING

SCIENCE

Second Edition 2024

Copyright @ Elemental Science, Inc.
Email: support@elementalscience.com

ISBN# 978-1-935614-42-5

Printed In USA For World Wide Distribution

For more copies write to:
Elemental Science
PO Box 79
Niceville, FL 32588
support@elementalscience.com

Table of Contents

Experiments   **Reading Plans**   **Notebooking**   **Activities**

Easy-to-use
SCIENCE PLANS
elemental**science**.com

1

The Three Keys to Science

Ilove science! But you might be surprised to know that it wasn't always that way for me.

In fact, I entered my very first chemistry class with much fear and trepidation. It was my sophomore year of high school. Many upperclassmen said chemistry was the most difficult class we would encounter.

I still remember hesitantly taking my seat that first day. After all, biology hadn't gone the way I had planned the previous year, and this class was supposed to be far worse. The uncertainty of the moment was causing my heart to clip along at a rapid pace. Glancing around at my classmates, I knew I wasn't the only one feeling that way.

The teacher waltzed to the rear of the room and shut off

the lights. The sound of a collective gasp of fear echoed off the concrete walls.

Whoosh – a Bunsen burner came to life at the back of the room.

All heads swiveled and were quickly captured by the sight of a glowing purple mass just above the flame. Not a sound could be heard as we waited to see what was next.

Fizz.

Bang.

Boom.

The glowing purple mass took flight!

It formed a shooting light trail that traveled from the back of the room before petering out at the front. We all let out a collective gasp, followed by oohing, as we watched the spectacle unfold.

Clip.

Clip.

Clip.

The teacher's heels rapped against the tile floor as she headed to the front of the room. She flipped on the lights, paused for our attention, and declared, "That was science!"

I think that my heart skipped a beat in anticipation of what she had in store. Thankfully, my teacher did not disappoint!

She told us how she had added a gummy bear to some sodium chlorate. How the heat from the Bunsen burner caused the sodium compound to melt. When the molten chemical met the gummy bear, it created an explosive reaction. That reaction sent the flaming gummy bear across the room.

She shared with us what the chemical reaction looked like. Then, she used that to explain what chemical equations should include and what they can tell us. She made sure to point out what we should be taking notes on. And finally, she gave us homework for that night that reinforced what we had learned in class.

That very first day, my chemistry teacher used all three of the keys for teaching science. She captured our interest with a scientific demonstration. She shared information with us. And she made sure that we kept a record of what we were learning.

Not every day in her class was as exciting as the first one, but I learned so much. I fell in love with chemistry that year and eventually went on to get a degree in Biochemistry.

What are the three keys to science?

I have studied science for years. I have taught science from preschool on up, both in the classroom and in homeschool groups. There are three essentials that I know must be included in each and every science plan. Each of these keys will help your students to gain a true understanding of the subject.

Key #1 – DO Science

The first key is to have the students do hands-on scientific tests. This will give them a chance to engage with the material they are learning, face to face, and to see science in action.

These scientific tests can be:

1. Teacher-led scientific demonstrations,
2. Student-performed experiments,
3. Nature studies,
4. Science fair projects, or
5. Interactive on-line demonstrations.

By doing regular hands-on scientific tests, the students see the concepts they are learning in action.

Key #2 – READ Science

The second key is to have the students gather information. In other words, they need to read about the science they have seen. This way, the students will learn more about the principles and concepts involved.

The students can read:

1. Standard textbooks,
2. Science-focused living books,
3. Non-fiction works, or
4. Age-appropriate encyclopedias.

By reading scientific information, the students are learning the information they need to know.

Key #3 – WRITE Science

The final key is to have the students write down what they have learned. They need to keep a record of the information they read about and what they did during their experiments.

The students can do this through:

1. Notebooking pages,
2. Comprehension worksheets,
3. Lapbooks, or
4. Lab reports and experiment sheets.

By writing down what they have learned, the students are organizing and sharing with others the facts they have studied.

A proven science curriculum will have students:

- DOING regular scientific tests,
- READING about science from reliable sources,
- and WRITING down what they have learned.

These three keys work together to provide a solid science education for your students.

A Final Thought

We'll dig deeper into these three keys in the coming chapters. Before we get started, I wanted to share one more thing about me with you—one of my life goals.

One of my biggest goals in life is to give homeschool teachers, like you, the tools you need to teach science. But not in the check-off-the-box-move-on-to-the-next-thing kind of way.

I want science to be the save-the-best-for-last kind of subject in your house. And when you use these three keys to formulate a customized plan for teaching science that fits your teaching style and your students' preferences, that is exactly what you will see.

2

Key #1 - DO Science

"Today we are going to do an experiment."

Did your heart skip a beat? Did you catch your breath? Or did your stomach do a flippity-flop after reading that statement?

Experiments have been long maligned and misunderstood. I have personally heard from many a homeschool mom the following statement:

> "I don't understand why experiments are even necessary. They are too much work and never turn out right, so we just don't do them."

My friends, it should not be so! Our students need to encounter science face-to-face. Experiments and other hands-on scientific tests are the tools we have to give our students this experience.

To teach science without the hands-on aspect would make no sense. It would be like a blind man watching a movie—it will sound right, but he really won't have a complete picture of what is going on.

Why do you need to do hands-on scientific tests?

Science is both a context and a content subject. It represents a beautiful partnership between facts and applications. If they are to fully understand science, our students need to know the information and see it in action.

I like to think of hands-on scientific tests as the flesh of the scientific facts your students are learning about. Adding these practical experiences with science will:

- Provide constructive reinforcement of the facts that the student is studying,

- Allow the students to interact with science face-to-face, and

- Show the students that science is more than just facts and figures.

In addition to serving as a visual reference of scientific fact, hands-on scientific tests foster scientific creativity and discovery in your students. You can show a set of plans for a popsicle-stick bridge to your students and talk them through the process, but that will most likely lead to glazed-over eyes and more than a few yawns. On the other hand, if you hand them a box with one hundred popsicle sticks, give them a few directions, and then let them loose, they are guaranteed to learn far more about the principles of engineering!

What are hands-on scientific tests?

We generally hear the word "experiments" used for all types of hands-on scientific tests, but the good news is that experiments are just one of the tools we can use to bring the hands-on aspect into our science teaching time.

Before I share the five main types of hands-on scientific tests that I prefer to use in the home-teaching setting, I would like to share with you all my definition of a hands-on scientific test:

> "A hands-on scientific test gives your student a chance to see, practice, test, or learn about a principle, or principles, in science."

In other words, hands-on scientific tests provide a visual reference of scientific information for your students.

Here are the five main types of scientific tests I regularly recommend using with your students:

1. **Scientific demonstrations** – These are teacher-led visual demonstrations of scientific facts.

2. **Experiments** – These are student-led explorations into scientific facts and theories.

3. **Nature studies** – These are outdoor excursions that seek to find scientific facts in nature.

4. **Science fair projects** – These are projects that employ the scientific method from start to finish.

5. **Interactive online demonstrations** – These demonstrations allow students to manipulate certain aspects of a scientific fact on their computer, such as those created by PhET.

You can use a combination of these scientific tests sprinkled throughout the year, or you can stick with the one that works the best for you. Either way, I recommend that you do at least one hands-on scientific test each week during the school year.

Which type of hands-on scientific tests should you do with your students?

The type of hands-on scientific tests you choose to do will depend largely on the students' ages.

Preschoolers will benefit the most from watching scientific demonstrations or doing nature walks.

Elementary students will benefit the most from moving from scientific demonstrations into doing experiments, or from doing nature study.

Middle and high school students will benefit the most from doing experiments, doing nature study, or playing with interactive online demonstrations. These students should also be completing yearly science fair projects.

Of course, this doesn't mean that you shouldn't do demonstrations with your high-schoolers – as they will certainly enjoy them.

Or that your elementary student should never, ever do a science fair project. If done correctly, the students will still learn from this type of project.

These suggestions are simply what will benefit different age groups the most.

Tips to maximize your success with hands-on scientific tests

Tip #1 – Have the materials on hand.

Whether you buy experiment kits or create your own, having the materials you need ready to go is a huge part of having success with hands-on scientific tests. After all, if you don't have the supplies you need, it will be virtually impossible to do the test you have planned to do.

Tip #2 – Plan Ahead.

It is a good idea to always read through the directions and explanations for the experiment, demonstration, or nature study you are planning on doing with your students. Knowing where you are going, what you are doing, and what you are trying to demonstrate is key to your success with hands-on scientific tests.

Tip #3 – Follow the directions.

Most of the directions for a scientific test are time-tested. The flow of the process is there for a reason, so it's worth following to ensure success with hands-on scientific tests.

Tip #4 – Discuss the explanation with your students.

You need to chat with your students about why the test you did worked, or why it didn't. Discussing with them what happened and why will help them to see and understand the scientific principles at work, which is the whole purpose of doing hands-on scientific tests.

3

Key #2 - READ Science

Ithink we can all agree that we need to teach our students about the principles, facts, and theories associated with science—although we might cringe a bit when we think about having to teach how to balance equations!

I don't know about you, but back in my day, the only way to learn about the "facts" of science was through textbooks or lectures. Most of which were dry, boring, and devoid of interesting visuals. I still managed to fall in love with the subject, thanks to encountering it face-to-face. But, I would like to suggest that, in this day and age, we can do better.

We have so many different tools at our fingertips that we can use to present the "facts" of science to our students. Before we get into that, though, let's cover the importance of providing a source of information gathering to our students.

Why do you need to gather information?

Science is more than experiments: There are principles that the students also need to know. Remember that science is both a context and a content subject—a marriage of facts and applications.

We need to teach our students the facts that have been proven to be true. We also need to provide them with an awareness of the theories that scientists are still studying.

As we gradually build their knowledge base over time, we provide the students with a knowledge base for further discovery. So, year by year, we want to be feeding our students with age-appropriate facts.

What can you use to gather information with your students?

There are lots of resources out there to help you present the facts and theories of science. Here are a few of my favorites:

1. **Science-focused living books** – We have enjoyed books like the *Burgess Bird Books, Madam How and Lady Why,* and *The Sassafras Science Adventures.*

2. **Age-appropriate encyclopedias** – We have used encyclopedias from publishers like DK, Usborne, and Kingfisher in our homeschool.

3. **Standard textbooks** – We use publishers like Prentice Hall and Miller & Levine when teaching

our high school courses.

4. **Current-events articles** – One of my go-to sources for these types of articles is Science News for Students.

5. **YouTube videos** – You can search for subject-specific videos or subscribe to certain channels, like NASA, Ted-Ed, and ACS Reactions, for weekly updates.

6. **Podcasts** – As podcasts grow in popularity, I am sure there will be more options, but right now, we really enjoy the Everyday Einstein podcast.

I recommend you read to your students or have the students read about science at least twice a week during the school year. However, the resources you use will depend upon your students' learning styles and your teaching preferences.

Some will prefer to read just the facts – textbooks, articles, and encyclopedias will fit the bill here.

Some will prefer a bit of excitement as they learn – living books, current events articles, and videos are a great option for this.

Some will prefer a more visual presentation – encyclopedias, videos, and library books will all work in this case.

In the early years, you will read to your children. As their reading skills increase, have your students read more and more on their own. (*Note—It is completely acceptable to keep the resources you use just below their reading level so that they can focus on the facts they are learning, rather than on the task of reading.*)

Tips for Gathering Information

Tip # 1 – Choose interesting resources.

You want to try to choose resources that will hold the interest of your students. Textbooks make some students groan and others swoon. In fact, I know of a student who slept with her textbook under her pillow at night! You can't always cater to the students' whims, but you should try frequently gathering information from resources they prefer.

Tip # 2 – Always discuss.

You want to chat with the students about what they have read. Discussing the material will help the students to assimilate the facts into their memory banks. Plus, it will also help to clear up any confusion they may have about the subject.

4
Key #3 - WRITE Science

So, at this point, we have led our students into encountering science face-to-face and we have fed them with the key facts, so we can stop there. Right?

Not so much. Think back to how many times you have said:

> "Hold on, let me write this down or I won't remember it."

My guess is that those times are probably too numerous to count. Well, the brains of our students, while quite a bit younger than ours, operate the same way. If they write it down, they are more likely to remember. In fact, research shows that students are 34% more likely to remember the information they are learning if they take the time to write it down.

So, if the simple act of writing down information increases

a person's ability to remember that data, we definitely need to incorporate that into our plan for science.

Let's explore a few more reasons why writing science, or rather keeping a record, is the third key to teaching science.

Why do you need to keep a record?

Keeping a record gives our students another chance to interact with the information. In other words, it provides them with another touch-point, which helps to firmly affix the material into their minds.

On top of that, writing it down also provides material for the student to review for testing or in future years. I can't count how many times we have pulled our daughter's old notebooks off the shelf to act as a reference and to start the journey down Memory Lane.

Over the years, I have been grateful that we have kept a record of what we have learned in science.

How do you keep a record?

You will have two streams of information to record from the first two keys.

- The students can record what they have done through their hands-on scientific tests, and

- The students can record the information they have gathered.

These two streams will be handled in different ways.

Recording hands-on scientific tests

Remember that hands-on scientific tests are very visual, which already helps to pin the information into the students' memories. However, it is beneficial to also have the students write down what they have learned while doing these tests. The method you use for hands-on scientific tests will depend largely upon the type of test you did.

Nature Journals

The nature journal is a personal record of what the student has learned during their nature study time. I generally recommend that you have the students record at least one scientific fact, along with the date and the place, on their nature journal page.

Demonstration or Lab Reports

Demonstration reports are simple records of what elementary students have seen and learned during a demonstration or experiment. These simple lab reports should include four sections:

1. **Our Tools** – This section will list the materials that were used during the demonstration.

2. **Our Method** – This section will contain the procedure for the demonstration, written in the student's own words.

3. **Our Outcome** – This section will contain what the students saw and record any data they have collected.

4. **Our Insight** – The final section of their lab report will contain a sentence or two about what the student has learned from the demonstration. Ideally, this will relate to the science being studied, but it is fine at this level for their sentences to be more superficial.

Experiment Sheets

Experiment sheets are more complete records of what the students have seen and done during an experiment. These experiment sheets should include the following sections:

1. **Title** – The title should be the question the students were attempting to answer or it should explain what they were observing.

2. **Hypothesis** – In this section, the students should share their prediction of the answer to the question posed in the lab. If the experiment is an observation, they can share what they think they will see or skip this section of the experiment sheet.

3. **Materials** – The materials section should contain a list of what the students used to complete the lab.

4. **Procedure** – In the procedure section, the students need to write a step-by-step account of what they did during their experiment. This should be a summary of what was done, written in their own words so that someone reading it would understand what occurred.

5. **Observations & Results** – In this section, the students will record what they observed during the experiment, as well as any data that they have collected.

6. **Conclusion** – Finally, in the conclusion section, the students will write whether or not their hypothesis was correct and will add any new information they learned from the lab. If their hypothesis was not correct, discuss why and have them include that on their lab report.

The detail the students include in the records will depend upon their age group. In other words, the older they are, the more detailed their nature journals and experiment sheets will be.

Recording information

The students will be gathering information through books and videos to learn about science. Having them record portions of this information will serve to solidify the facts in their minds. You can use:

- Oral Narration and Dictation,

- Notebooking,

- Lapbooks,

- Comprehension worksheets,

- List of Facts,

- Outlines, or

- Sketches.

What method you use and how many times you record information each week will depend upon your students' ages.

In the early years, you can use oral narration, notebooking, and lapbooks several times a week. The students will not actually write much in the beginning, but they will increase the amount with their abilities.

As they mature, you can use notebooking, comprehension worksheets, lists of facts, outlines, and sketches. Again, the amount they write will increase with their abilities.

I personally love notebooking and have seen great success using this method of recording information in our homeschool. The three main reasons I prefer notebooking over comprehension worksheets are:

Reason #1 - Notebooking requires the students to think about what they have learned.

In other words, there are no canned responses in notebooking. There are no blanks to fill in. There are no answers to match up. Instead, the students need to mull over what they just read to formulate a summary of what they learned. In short, notebooking requires that the students engage with the material before they write down a word.

Reason #2 - Notebooking provides freedom for the students.

This freedom from the "I have to get the right answer" syndrome allows the students to write about what they find to be meaningful, which means they are more likely to remember the information. Notebooking allows the freedom for the student to write down the most interesting and meaningful facts they found in what they read.

Reason #3 -Notebooking engages both sides of the students' brains.

Notebooking has two key components—the material content and the visual component. The material content is what the students write, while the visual component is a picture that relates to the topic. The two pieces stimulate different parts of the brain, which helps to solidify the information in their minds.

But enough about the benefits of notebooking. Let's wrap this chapter up with a few tips for succeeding with the third key for teaching science.

Tips for succeeding at keeping a record

Tip #1 - Make it easy.

In other words, don't push your students to write beyond their abilities in science. You don't want your students to end up hating science simply because they have to write it down. The writing you do in science should reinforce what your students have already learned to do in writing.

Tip #2 - Make it fun.

Switch up the type of writing you require. In one unit you can have them do a notebooking page, the next unit you can have them make a lapbook. Changing the type of writing you require can keep things fun and fresh.

Tip #3 - Make it visual.

Add cut-out pictures, photos, or drawings to provide another connection to the material for your students. Plus, it makes their work interesting and appealing to share with others!

5

The Fun Extras—Crafts and More!

Now that we have covered the three keys for teaching science, I wanted to share some of the fun extras you can add to your week! These are things like crafts and projects that are super fun and can make us look like rock star moms.

That is, unless you are a mom like me, and the thought of having to vacuum up glitter for weeks on end sets you firmly in the non-crafty mom camp. Don't worry, I've got some ideas for extras that your kids will enjoy that won't make you want to run out of the room screaming.

Why should you bother with extras?

First, let's chat about why we should even bother with the extras—they are optional, after all. Things like crafts, projects, and posters are not part of the three essential keys for teaching science, so why should you even bother with them in the first place?

Well, all those extras can:

- Feed the student's passion for learning science,
- Fuel the fire of learning you have sparked with the three keys, and
- Support and reinforce what the student is studying.

In short, the extras spice things up and keep the students interested in learning about science.

What can you use as extras?

What exactly constitutes an "extra?" Here is my definition:

> "An extra is something that adds to or enhances what the students are already learning in their core curriculum."

In science, extras can include the following:

- Memory work,
- Field trips,
- Crafts,
- Posters, or
- Science activities.

Let's take a closer look at each of these.

Memory work

You can have the students work on memorizing fun, fact-filled poems, silly songs, or lists of facts related to what you are studying. The point here is to choose facts that you want them to remember for years to come, like the fact that mammals have hair.

Field Trips

You can go for a hike to look for the rocks you are studying. You can head to the zoo to learn more about animals. You can go to a bakery to learn more about the chemistry of food. You can visit your local science museum. The field trip possibilities are endless!

Crafts

You can add related art projects, like making edible Jell-O cells, sculpting clay earth models, or drawing azaleas with chalk pastels. You can even pull out the glitter to decorate a model comet.

Posters

You can have the students make informational posters, such as one about the life cycle of a star, one showing the periodic table, or one about the metamorphosis of a butterfly. You can also have them make posters that compare two topics, like renewable resources and non-renewable resources, or acids and bases.

Science Activities

You can do another experiment related to the topic, or something that is just pure fun, like magnetic slime! You can also add in a citizen science project, like the Great Backyard Bird Count or a recycling project.

You certainly do not need to add each and every one of these ideas every week. Instead, you can add some memory work when you land on a subject the students can't get enough of. You can take a field trip to reinforce what you are teaching. Or, you can throw in a craft when you find your students are bored with the normal routine.

6

Choosing a Science Curriculum

So, now that we have discussed the key components of your plan for science, how do you find a curriculum that has those keys and fits your family's situation?

As homeschoolers, many of us adhere to a certain learning philosophy, such as classical or interest-led. These methods give us a basic framework for choosing curricula, but it can still be a challenge to find the one specific curriculum that fits your particular family.

Every homeschooling family is unique. We have different overall educational goals. Our students have their own learning styles. And our sequence of study may not match every other member of the homeschooling community at large. All this means that no one homeschool science curriculum can fit every situation, which has led to the multitude of options we have access to in the market today.

So how do you wade through all of the choices?

It is a simple matter of knowing what you are looking for before you begin your search.

I know—that's clear as muddy water! Let's filter out a few key steps you need to take before you type that first keyword in the Google search bar.

Step #1 - Determine your goals.

As with any homeschool subject, you need to first determine your goals for teaching science. Ask yourself…

What do I have to prepare my students for?

For instance, if you plan on preparing a student for college, it's good to know what science he will be required to complete in high school. That way, you can begin to introduce those subjects much earlier.

What do I want to instill in my students about science?

We all have those ideals that we want our students to have engrained in their hearts before leaving our homes. For science, examples could be, "I want my students to fall in love with nature" or "I want my students to get excited about science."

Is there anything that you must teach your students?

For instance, if you plan on sending your homeschooled students back to a regular school the following year, you need to make sure that they are prepared to go to the particular school in time.

It's good to have both realistic long-range and short-range goals—things that you are shooting to complete by the end of your students' homeschooling journeys and things that you want to complete by the end of the year.

I highly recommend writing out these goals. Then, keep them in your homeschool binder to refer back to on those days when you need to refind your compass. Or for those days when you need to be encouraged that you are heading in the right direction.

Step #2 - Know your students' learning styles.

It is important to understand how each of your students prefer to learn. This way, you can choose a science curriculum that will maximize your teaching efforts.

A student can have one type of learning style across the board or they can blend several types to create their own style. There are four basic learning styles:

1. **Visual** – These students need to see things before they pick up on the information.

2. **Auditory** – These students learn best from hearing, either from read-alouds, lectures, or discussions.

3. **Tactile** – These students need to touch things. They acquire information best from tangible processes.

4. **Kinesthetic** – These students learn best when they are moving.

As your students get older, you do need to stretch them by teaching them how to learn from materials that are outside of their preferred learning mode.

I will also add that you can alter most science curricula to fit your students' learning styles. However, it helps to know this information before choosing, since not all curricula can be easily molded to fit each of your particular students.

Step #3 - Decide how you would prefer to learn.

You have written out your goals. You know your students' learning styles. Now you need to determine how you as a family prefer to learn. Do you love to sit around the table together, examining nature or reading from an interesting book? Or do you prefer to have your students take the lead in their own individualized learning journey?

It is far easier to determine how you should go about studying science once you have a picture of how you prefer learning to look in your homeschool. You can ask yourself the following questions to help create your image:

1. **Would we prefer to learn about science from a textbook, encyclopedia, or living book?** If you prefer a "just the facts" approach, textbooks or encyclopedias will work well for your situation. If you prefer to have an adventure as you learn, check out living books!

2. **Would we prefer to learn about science outdoors or through indoor scientific tests?** For example, those who prefer learning outdoors will do very well with a curriculum that promotes nature study.

3. **Would we prefer to learn about science through notebooking or through worksheets?** I have written about the benefits of notebooking before, but some students will thrive on a "just the fact" worksheet-style approach.

4. **Would we prefer to enrich our science study time with hands-on learning projects?** A craft project is a great way to reinforce what a student is learning, but it can also lead some students towards frustration, which is not conducive to learning science.

5. **Would we enjoy spending one year on one area of science or would we prefer to pick and choose units?** Within an area of science, like biology, you can jump around on topics, such as animals, plants, and the human body. Even so, it is also acceptable to do a little biology, a little physics, and a little earth science, all in one year.

Knowing what your masterpiece for learning would look like will help you to determine which science curriculum will best fit your needs.

Step #4 - Choose what you would like to study.

So, we have laid a lot of groundwork for understanding your homeschool's unique profile. Now, we need to work out a few nitty-gritty details before searching for the science curriculum that will best fit your home's academy.

Sometimes, your learning philosophy will help you to choose what to study. Other times, your students will determine what they would like to learn for the year. Either way, you can ask yourself two questions to help determine what to look for in a homeschool science curriculum:

What would I like to see my students learn this year?

Your learning philosophy may already have set guidelines for what to teach each year or you may have certain benchmark concepts that you would like your students to know by a specific time. Writing out what (if anything) you want your students to learn in a particular year will help you determine which curriculum to choose.

What would my students like to study this year?

It is perfectly acceptable, and rather common in the homeschooling world, to ask your students what they would like to learn. After all, if they are interested in the subject matter, they will be more likely to engage with the materials and retain the information that they are studying.

Now that you have both broad and focused ideas of what a science curriculum needs to have to fit into your homeschool, it is time to begin the search!

But, I don't want to leave you there. Here are five questions to help you as you wade through those search results.

Questions to Ask as You Evaluate the Curriculum Options

1. Does this curriculum cover what we want to learn about this year?

A good place to start your search is with what you plan on learning for the year.

2. Does this curriculum have the three keys?

Look for weekly hands-on scientific tests, along with bi-weekly ways of gathering information and keeping records.

3. Does this curriculum fit my goals?

A curriculum may be the best thing since sliced bread according to the community at large, but if it does not support your education goals for your children, it is perfectly acceptable to keep searching.

4. Will this curriculum work for my students' learning styles?

Of course, you can manipulate any curriculum to perfectly fit each of your students, but if one is a visual/tactile learner, a curriculum that is centered around a black-and-white textbook probably won't work for that situation.

5. Does this curriculum look like something we will enjoy?

After all, you want science to be enjoyable, not something you have to slog through each week!

Appendix

Resources to Explore

So, there you have it—the three keys to teaching science. Of course, you can always add in fun projects, crafts, and activities to support the basics, but a good science plan should always have the following three fundamentals:

- DO Science

- READ Science

- WRITE Science

These three keys will give you the tools for unlocking the science-learning potential found deep within your students.

I want to leave you with a list of articles that I have written, which you can dig into to learn more about the concepts and methods introduced in this book. Instead of sharing every single one here, you can see all these links in one easy-to-click place at:

⌖ http://elementalscience.com/pages/3-keys-articles

Before you go...

Can you help us spread the word?

If you enjoyed this book, please take a few moments to write a review of it. Here are a few places you can find it:

- Elemental Science Website

- Amazon

- Goodreads

Thank you!

elemental science

Are you looking for a science program with the three keys?

At Elemental Science, all of our programs contain the three keys for teaching science, plus a few extras, all wrapped up in easy-to-use packages just for you!

1. DO Science: Each of our programs has weekly hands-on experiments or demonstrations, with step-by-step instructions, the expected results, and clear explanations. We also offer experiment kits to make gathering the supplies easy on you!

2. READ Science: Each of our programs contains day-by-day reading plans that will teach the students the facts they need to know. Depending upon the series, your students will be reading from living books or encyclopedias.

3. WRITE Science: Each of our programs includes customized notebooking pages and experiment sheets to help the students organize and share what they have learned. In the end, you will have a beautiful scrapbook of what the students have learned with minimal effort!

Visit elementalscience.com or keep reading to learn more.

Classical
SCIENCE

The programs in the Classical Science series are full-year-long programs, meaning they contain 36 weeks of plans for you to use. They cover a single broad discipline per year - biology, earth science and astronomy, chemistry, or physics.

Here are how the three keys work in these programs...

1. **DO Science:** Weekly demonstrations or experiments found in the teacher guides.

2. **READ Science:** Readings come from full-color, visually appealing children's non-fiction books by publishers such as DK, Kingfisher, or Usborne.

3. **WRITE Science:** Custom notebook with plenty of pictures and space to write down what they have learned. (There are also optional lapbooks and coloring pages with the grammar stage programs.)

The programs in this series also include...

4. **Optional Extras:** Memory work, vocabulary, and additional STEAM activities, plus review sheets for the grammar stage and tests for the logic stage.

See our award-winning classical science programs at:

✆ https://elementalscience.com/collections/classical-science

The main programs in the Sassafras Science series are semester-long programs, meaning they contain 18 weeks of plans for you to use. The novels cover a single area of science per year - zoology, anatomy, botany, earth science, geology, astronomy, chemistry, and physics.

Here are how the three keys work in these programs...

1. **DO Science:** Weekly demonstrations are included in the activity guides for the teacher.

2. **READ Science:** Readings come from the included text - either the stories in Summer's Lab or the Sassafras Science Adventure novels.

3. **WRITE Science:** Custom notebook with plenty of pictures and space to write down what they have learned. (There are also optional lapbooks and coloring pages with the programs.)

The programs in this series also include...

4. **Optional Extras:** Memory work, vocabulary, and additional STEAM activities, plus quizzes for each of the locations in the novels.

Start your adventure with the Sassafras Twins here:

🖱 https://elementalscience.com/collections/sassafras-science

The programs in the Science Chunks series are 4 to 12-week-long units. However, we also have year bundles with 36 weeks of plans for you to use. The idea is that you will cover multiple disciplines through several units each year. In other words, you'll do a bit of biology, a bit of earth science or astronomy, a bit of chemistry, and a bit of physics each year.

Here are how the three keys work in these units...

1. **DO Science:** Weekly demonstrations or hands-on science activities are included in the guide.

2. **READ Science:** Readings come from full-color, visually appealing children's non-fiction books by publishers such as DK, Kingfisher, or Usborne.

3. **WRITE Science:** Custom lapbook templates and notebooking pages with plenty of pictures and space to write down what they have learned.

The programs in this series also include...

4. **Optional Extras:** Additional STEAM activities, vocabulary, and review sheets.

Pick and choose your science units:

☝ https://elementalscience.com/collections/science-chunks

About the Author

Hi-ya! I am Paige Hudson, which you probably already know since it is on the front cover of this book! I wanted to share a few things about myself with you so that you can get to know me a bit.

I first discovered my love of science during a high school chemistry course, during the now infamous gummy bear incident, which I wrote about in this first chapter. That love led to a major in Biochemistry at Virginia Tech.

Several years after graduation, a marriage to my best friend in the whole wide world, and the miracle of becoming a mom later, I began writing a science curriculum. At first, it was just for our beautiful daughter to use, but with a little vision from my husband and a lot of elbow grease from us both, one curriculum has grown into a full company—Elemental Science.

My passion remains to see all students enjoy and excel in their pursuit of sciences. These days, you can find me writing from our home in between homeschooling our two kids. In my spare time (those of you who are homeschool moms can feel free to snicker at the idea of "spare time"), I love to read, cook, and hike with my husband and two children.

www.ingramcontent.com/pod-product-compliance
Lightning Source LLC
Chambersburg PA
CBHW060627030426
42337CB00018B/3241